Saving the World in Your Spare Time

The Pocket Guide to Effecting Positive Change

Laura Klotz

PublishAmerica

Baltimore

First printing

ISBN: 1-59286-508-9
PUBLISHED BY PUBLISHAMERICA, LLLP
www.publishamerica.com
Baltimore

Printed in the United States of America

Acknowledgements

A book like this is not easy to write. I would have found it even more difficult without the help and inspiration of many people:

My husband, Kevin, who not only was the book's first reader and fan, but who also kept me fed during the hours I spent hunched over the keyboard;

My mother and stepfather, Debbie and Ravi, who frequently provide me with great inspiration on this particular subject;

My sisters, Lisa and Liza, who each make their own valuable contributions to the betterment of our world;

My grandparents, Edmund and Lucille, who have always regarded "Laura's writing" as a matter of greater importance than it really deserved;

My church's leaders, Pastor Gary and Linda Walbert, who have introduced me to countless new ways to be involved; and

My best friend Jessica, who encouraged this idea from its first germination.

If I attempted to list all the friends and relations who deserve inclusion here, the acknowledgements would be longer than the book. So I hope you'll forgive me if I just group you all together and lob one gigantic "thank you" in your general direction. Your love, support, encouragement, and tolerance over the years merit more gratitude than I'm able to express in a few lines.

Finally, I most certainly wish to thank Marie Raeder of the Acquisitions Department, and all the people at PublishAmerica, for giving this book the chance to make a difference.

L. K. K
December 2002

Table of Contents

Introduction

"The world is going to hell in a hand basket."

How many times have you heard this sentiment, or something like it? It's becoming a more and more common philosophy in these troubling times: The world has gone absolutely crackers, and there's nothing we can do about it. Look at the events of September 11, 2001. When humans can do something like that to each other, what hope is there for any of us?

The answer to that question is to look past 9-11. What happened on that terrible day was the very worst kind of crime against humanity; you'll get no argument from me on that score. But don't just look at that day's events—look past them to the events of the subsequent days and weeks. Out of the very worst of human behavior came some of the very best. Has there ever been another time like that, when so many good people understood that they had to join together to fight against evil? Even though that evil didn't yet have a name or a face, we fought against it. Hands reached out to help. Supplies for the volunteer workers flew off the shelves in a frenzy of generosity. Blood banks actually had to turn people away because they had too *much* blood.

Unfortunately, as is so often the case, the initial enthusiasm ebbed away. The overwhelming pain and shock and sadness gradually turned into a numbness, then an acceptance of what had happened. People had thrown themselves into a great display of goodwill in order to soothe their own suffering; once the suffering eased, they didn't have to work so hard.

The only thing necessary for evil to succeed is for good people to do nothing.

I believe in my heart that most people are good. (I absolutely have to believe this, or I will never be able to turn on the news again.) I think a lot more people would be willing to do good things if they thought they could actually make a difference. It's hard to be convinced that we can do anything to make the world better when a child takes a gun to school and kills a classmate, or another bomb gets sent through the mail.

A bumper sticker on a car in my local mall's parking lot reads "Practice random kindnesses and senseless acts of beauty." It's a great sentiment, but expressed poorly. Pull it apart to see what I mean. "Random kindnesses" —why must they be random? Shouldn't we set out to be deliberately kind to each other? "Senseless acts of beauty" is a senseless phrase; an act of beauty, by definition, is not senseless. More to the point, "Practice random kindnesses and senseless acts of beauty" has never inspired me to do anything. It gives me no idea of how to go about fulfilling its lofty goal.

I'm hoping to do better with this book.

I've often heard people say things like "I don't have the time to volunteer" or "I can't afford to make a donation." But what a lot of us don't seem to realize is that there really is no such thing as an action too small. No matter what you do, you're going to have an impact somewhere. Dropping a quarter into a collection jar by the grocery store cash register seems like a completely insignificant thing, but to the people collecting that money, every little bit helps.

If you've picked up this book, you've taken the first step. Clearly, you are someone who wants to do something to make the world a better place. Congratulations on having that initiative! I hope I don't fail you in your quest to find a way to help.

This world is a remarkable place, for all that it is a "fixer-upper" of sorts. It's filled with so many different kinds of people, and yet the truth of the matter is that we aren't all that different. Issues like crime, poverty, environmental destruction, disease, and prejudice don't stop at any national border. They transcend every known distinction, from gender to religion to color to class. Whether we admit it or not, we are all affected by the problems of others. Therefore, we all have a responsibility to do *something*.

We can't all perform great actions of change. Not everyone has the money, or the clout, or the political power. But we can effect small changes…and small changes have a way of growing into big changes. For instance, if every single person in the United States contributed just one penny, there would be well over *three million dollars* with which we could do so much good. Three million dollars would preserve thousands of acres of rain forests…feed hundreds of hungry children…provide extra funding for our public schools…or allow us to do any number of other great things.

How do you plan to spend *your* pennies?

Chapter One—The Workbook

Before we take a look at the ideas in this book, you should get an idea about yourself. What do you most want to change in this world? How can you make the most difference with your individual beliefs and talents?

There are no right or wrong answers to these questions. It's very important for you to understand that. This "test" is really just a way to get your own thoughts going. It's set up to help you figure out the best way for you to get involved. Would you be more effective as part of an organization, or on your own? Would you rather volunteer on a regular basis, or set up projects when your schedule allows? Although you'll find my list of ideas in the next chapter, I'm hoping that by answering these questions thoughtfully and honestly, you'll be able to come up with your own ideas for projects to make the world better. I've left spaces where you can write your answers, as well as make notes of anything that comes to you along the way.

1. When volunteering, would you feel comfortable being told what to do, or would you rather decide for yourself?

---

2. How flexible is your schedule (work, school, etc.)? Can you fit in a regular project—for instance, every week on the same afternoon—or would it be easier for you to just do what you can, when you can?

_____

_____

3. Would you rather do something as part of a team, or are you more comfortable with a solo project?

_____

_____

4. Given the choice, would you rather work with:
- kids or adults? _____
- people or animals? _____

5. Would you rather do something physical, like picking up litter, or something more mental, such as circulating petitions?

_____

_____

6. Are you more concerned about the human condition (diseases, poverty, etc.) or about the planet (deforestation, pollution, etc.)? If you consider yourself equally concerned about both, list one thing you'd be willing to do to help each cause:

_____

_____

7. Are you at ease performing your volunteer work in an environment strongly influenced by religion, or would you prefer

to work in a more secular environment (no particular religious affiliation)?

_____

_____

8. Do you feel comfortable asking others to donate money for a cause, or would you rather do something that doesn't require you to solicit donations?

_____

_____

9. Do you have your own transportation (car, bus pass, bicycle), or will you have to rely on someone else to get you to your project? How far are you—or they—willing to travel?

_____

_____

10. Are you a legal adult (18 in most areas)? Does your planned activity have any kind of age restriction? If you aren't an adult, will you need to have your parent or guardian sign a consent form or anything like that?

_____

_____

All done? Pencils down.

Now that you've had some time to think about these considerations, let's go over what the different questions and your answers mean.

1. *When volunteering, would you feel comfortable being told what to do, or would you rather decide for yourself?* I listed this question first because it's one of the most important things to

consider. If you don't like taking direction from someone else, you might not feel comfortable being involved with an organization. When you volunteer with an established organization, you'll be assigned specific tasks and usually told exactly how to do them. If you're okay with that kind of setup, that's great, but if you aren't, you're going to want to look for an alternative to organized volunteering.

2. *How flexible is your schedule?* This is also really important, especially if you're planning to volunteer with a group or club. You may be required to attend weekly meetings, a monthly seminar, or some other regular event. Some people with erratic schedules—for example, retail employees who don't work the same hours every day—might have a harder time planning a recurring activity. Another thing you need to consider when making plans like this is your family; do you have children who will need a baby-sitter? Are your volunteer plans going to interfere with some family activity? Some people's schedules are more open than others, so if you want to do your good works as part of a group, try to find partners or team members whose own plans coordinate well with your own. Otherwise, consider going with a solo project that lets you arrange things at your leisure.

3. *Would you rather do something as part of a team, or are you more comfortable with a solo project?* This question is simply about personal preferences. Some people function best when left to their own devices. Others find that working with others helps them to stay focused and inspired. This is totally a matter of what works best for you, and how that should impact what you decide to do.

4. *Given the choice, would you rather work with:*

- *kids or adults?* Some people love children and would enjoy doing a volunteer project that involves them. Others don't have the patience that working with children requires. There's also the option of working with older children, such as in a program for teenagers; the kids still need adult guidance, but you don't have to change diapers. Still, if you don't enjoy the company of kids, or don't think you'll be able to handle them, you'd be better off volunteering in another capacity.

- *people or animals?* I know some people who really prefer the company of animals over that of other people! Even if that's not your case, animal lovers will enjoy taking on projects where they can help their furry, feathered, or finned friends. But if you have allergies, or just aren't an animal fancier, you should probably stick to your own species.

5. *Would you rather do something physical, like picking up litter, or something more mental, such as circulating petitions?* A lot of volunteer projects are physically demanding. It takes strength and endurance to help build a new shelter or participate in a fundraiser walk-a-thon. If you don't really enjoy physical activity, or are unable to do things like that for medical reasons, you'll want to look into projects where you can make use of other skills and abilities.

6. *Are you more concerned about the human condition or about the planet?* This question was designed to make you think about which causes you truly want to support. Would you rather attend an AIDS fundraiser, or raise money to preserve acres of rain forest? Are you more interested to contributing canned goods to a soup kitchen, or writing letters to lawmakers about keeping our oceans clean? You can, incidentally, be equally concerned about both issues; you'll just have to think harder about what you want to do

about them.

7. *Are you at ease performing your volunteer work in an environment strongly influenced by religion, or would you prefer to work in a more secular environment?* Many volunteer opportunities are available through houses of worship, as well as through religion-oriented groups like the Salvation Army. If you have strong religious convictions yourself, and would enjoy working with a group that shares your feelings, you might want to consider looking into opportunities like these. If you don't think you'd be comfortable in that situation, however, you might want to look elsewhere for ideas.

8. *Do you feel comfortable asking others to donate money for a cause, or would you rather do something that doesn't require you to solicit donations?* This is another important consideration for you to make when deciding how to help. If you want to be involved with an organization, you need to remember that what most nonprofit groups need more than anything else (besides volunteers) is money. They might not be making it, but they usually need to spend it in order to work toward fulfilling their mission. So a lot of volunteers spend time on the phone or stuffing envelopes, asking people to contribute money for their cause; others recruit sponsors for participants in charity marathons and other events. If you aren't comfortable doing this, make that clear before you're asked to do it, or else look for volunteer opportunities that let you do other things.

9. *Do you have your own transportation, or will you have to rely on someone else to get you to your project? How far are you—or they—willing to travel?* If you don't have access where you live to the kinds of projects you want to do, you're going to

need to find a way to get where you want to go. If you drive, make a realistic decision as to how far you're willing to go (and how much you're willing to spend on gas) to do your volunteering. If you rely on public transportation, you'll need to take that into consideration when scheduling your volunteer work; for example, some cities don't run their buses after a certain hour, so you'll want to be done with your work before the last bus leaves. If you're going to be getting a ride with someone else, are they going to be willing to provide you with a ride as often as you need one? Will you need to pay them for their gas, or reimburse them in some other way? All of these factors must be determined before you make any kind of formal commitment to a project.

10. *Are you a legal adult?* This is really a lot more important than some people might realize. More kids and teenagers are involved with volunteering today than ever before, and it's a wonderful thing. They bring energy and enthusiasm to the volunteer projects, and often inspire each other to stay involved. The problem with underage volunteering is that some programs and organizations don't want to be held responsible for anything that might happen to someone else's child. Parental consent forms are usually required for any formal volunteer project performed by kids or teens, so if you're not of the "age of consent," make sure you get one signed. If your volunteering isn't with an organization—for example, you and a few friends want to clean up a polluted stream one afternoon—you should still always get your parent or guardian's permission before you get started. They'll want to know where you're going to be, and may have other safety concerns. They may also know things you don't, like that your stream cleanup project will take you onto private property. Besides, you never know—they just might offer to come along and help!

Chapter Two—My Idea List

As I said in the introduction, I think a lot more people would get out and help if they only knew what to do. So I started thinking about things that people *could* do. I didn't want to just list big projects that required a team effort; I also wanted to include "little" things, ideas that wouldn't require a whole lot of time or energy, but would still make a difference somewhere. People have very busy lives, so I wanted to make sure I had projects listed that would fit easily into hectic schedules. You'll be surprised at the kinds of things you can squeeze into a day or even just an hour. All that any of them really require are the willingness to try. Many of these suggestions refer to specific groups and organizations; you'll find contact information for those in Chapter Five. A few items on the list aren't ideas for projects at all; rather, they are suggestions for small changes you can make to your lifestyle which will have a positive impact on the world.

Some of these ideas may seem extremely unimportant on a large scale; for instance, my ideas for helping your neighbors don't sound like much that will change the world. But every little bit really does make it better. There's a story about a little boy and his grandfather walking down a beach; the tide had gone out, leaving hundreds of starfish stranded on the sand. The little boy kept picking them up and throwing them back into the water. His grandfather asked him, "Why do you bother? You can't save them all, you know. What difference can it possibly make?" The little grandson, with his knees caked with sand and his eyes bright, held up a starfish and replied, "It makes a difference to *this* one!" Then he turned and threw it into the sea.

I'm not expecting anyone to go out and do all of these things; I know I've never done all of them. Just pick out one that you think you can handle, one that you can fit into your own routine, and give it a try. It's amazing how good it feels. Don't be surprised if you find yourself trying a second suggestion before too long!

Help Your Friends and Neighbors

~ New neighbors moving in? Be a one-person welcome wagon. Take over a casserole or a dessert for the family and introduce yourself. You could also bring the newcomers a map of the area and let them know where to find necessities like grocery stores and gas stations, as well as local attractions. Make sure to include them on the invite list for the next block party or neighborhood get-together, so they can start to feel like part of the community.

~ Set aside an afternoon and drop in on someone whom you know doesn't get much company. Go out and see a movie, stay in and play checkers, or just give them a friendly ear. When someone is lonely, a few hours can mean so much.

~ Let your neighbors know you care. If someone has a new baby, is caring for a sick relative, or suffers a loss in their family, your kindness can be a great relief. During times of great stress like those, even the smallest tasks can seem overwhelming. Volunteer to make dinner, baby-sit, run errands, or mow the lawn.

~ Join or establish a neighborhood watch in your town. These groups send volunteers out in teams of two and three to walk around town and keep an eye out for crimes in progress; they carry two-way radios with which to contact police. Criminals rely on your silence to help them carry out their illegal acts, so get your neighbors involved and help protect each other.

~ Teach someone to read. This is an extremely involved project, requiring a lot of patience and dedication on your part, but if you can handle it, it's a very important service to provide. Illiteracy plays a big part in many of today's problems, including global overpopulation and drug addiction. Your local library can refer you to a literacy program, or you can contact the Literacy Volunteers of America for more information.

~ Spread a little joy. Smile and say thank you to your waitress, the cashier at the grocery store, the bus driver. It never hurts to brighten someone's day just a tiny bit—and as J. M. Barrie (the author of *Peter Pan*) said, "Those who bring sunshine to the lives of others cannot keep it from themselves."

Help People You Don't Know

~ Read about the issues and difficulties facing the world today. Be it poverty, violence, or crime, it's always easier to find a solution when you fully understand the problem.

~ Roll up your sleeve and donate blood. It only takes about an hour, and a single donation can save as many as three lives. Bonus—free cookies!

~ If you're old enough and you haven't already, register to vote. If you are registered, do your best to be at the polls every election day. Use the power of your vote to elect people who will make a difference, and to remove from office the ones who don't. This goes for every issue, from caring for our senior citizens to protecting wildlife.

~ When you're out doing your holiday shopping, pick up a few new stuffed toys, board games, or dolls for a child you don't know. These don't have to be expensive; go with what you can afford. Donate your purchases to the Marine Corps' Toys for Tots drive, or to a local hospital to be given to sick children.

~ Locate the nearest drop-off point for donations to your area's food bank. Try calling city hall or a nearby church for this information. Find out which items they need most, and add one of these to your grocery shopping list every week. If your community doesn't have a food bank, consider petitioning the local government to start one.

~ Keep a jar on your bookshelf, dresser, or some other place where you can see it every day. Whenever you pass the jar, empty your pockets of any loose change you happen to be carrying. Once the jar is full, count up the coins and donate the amount to charity. If you live near a store with a CoinStar machine, that's even better—the machine will sort and count the coins for you, set them aside for the charity you select onscreen, and print a receipt for you to file with your income taxes.

~ If you've got long hair and are thinking of cutting it shorter, consider donating the cropped tresses to Locks of Love. This organization takes the hair and turns it into wigs, which are then given to children who have lost their own hair due to medical problems.

~ Instead of tossing out last month's magazines, give them a new home. Nursing homes often accept the reading material to distribute to their residents, as do some hospitals. Many schools and day care facilities also accept the magazines to be cut up for craft projects.

~ Call your local soup kitchen and offer to help serve meals. Do it one time or once a week, it's up to you. But here's a side tip: these establishments often have a plethora of volunteers during Thanksgiving and the December holidays, when people are brimming with generosity. You might consider volunteering your services during other times of the year, when they need help more.

~ Clean out your closet. Pull out all the clothes that don't fit anymore, that you don't like, or that you haven't worn in at least a year. Bag them up and donate them to a clothing drive for charity—or start one yourself with your friends and family. Organizations like Goodwill and the Salvation Army always accept donations of used clothing in good condition.

~ The next time you renew your driver's license, sign up to be an organ donor. Lives are being lost every day because people need replacement organs and there just aren't enough for everyone; you can elect to donate tissue, blood, and bone marrow as well. You can also sign and carry an organ donor's card in your purse or wallet. Make sure to discuss this decision with your family, so they know what your specific wishes are.

~ Collect used cellular phones. So many people today use cell phones, and some have old ones they no longer use. Motorola and the Wireless Foundation are collecting these used phones and reprogramming them, then distributing them to victims of domestic violence so they always have a way to phone for help. Ask the cell phone users in your life to contribute their old phones to this program; make sure they've deactivated the service on the phones first, then send them to the Wireless Foundation.

~ If you or somebody in your family wears glasses, you more than likely have a couple of old pairs that no longer fit or have an outdated prescription. The members of Lions Club International collect these old glasses and match them to needy people who can't afford new ones. Contact your local chapter to find out where to drop off your specs. The Lions also collect used crutches, walkers, hearing aids, and lots of other things; if you aren't sure about a specific item, just ask. They'll even arrange to pick the items up at your house if you can't come to them.

~ Every year, especially during the holiday season, people receive dozens of beautiful cards from friends and family members all over the world. Most of these end up in the trash or, at best, get recycled. But there's an even better option available. St. Jude's Ranch is a home for abused, neglected, and abandoned children. When you send your used greeting cards to the ranch, the kids turn them into brand-new cards, which they then sell to earn money for college.

~ Food For All is a multinational organization looking to put an end to world hunger. You can help them—all you have to do is go grocery shopping! At many stores and supermarkets, you'll find cards at the checkout labeled with different monetary amounts. Pick up a card in the amount you'd like to donate and add it to your purchases; the store will add the amount to your total, then pass your donation on to the organization.

~ Seek out your local chapter of Habitat for Humanity and help them in their quest to build houses for the homeless. You can be a regular volunteer or just go along on a single project. You can even get a group of your friends together to help and have a volunteer party!

Help Our Animal Friends

~ Adopt a pet from your local animal shelter. There are two kinds of shelters—those who put the animals to sleep after a certain period of time (in order to reduce crowding), and those who don't. If you adopt from a euthanizing shelter, you'll save the animal's life; if you adopt from a no-kill shelter, you'll be freeing up space and resources for them to take in another stray. So either way, you're doing something really good—and you're also getting a wonderful new friend.

~ A big reason why so many animal shelters are overcrowded is because too many pet owners don't spay or neuter their cats and dogs. The pet population is too high. Spaying and neutering your animal friends is a safe way to help reduce the number of homeless animals, and these procedures also make for more well-behaved pets.

~ If you love animals but can't have pets for one reason or another, call your local shelter and ask about volunteer opportunities. Animal shelters often need caring people to help nurse injured animals, bathe them, clean cages, and fulfill various other tasks. They'll probably be willing to accept any help you could give them.

~ Vegetarianism is a very animal-friendly way to eat, but not everyone is into the idea. If you'd like to be a more critter-conscious diner without giving up meat entirely, consider cutting veal and lobster from your diet. Veal comes from calves who spend their whole short lives confined in crates, while lobsters are cooked by dropping the live animals into pots of boiling water.

~ If you see a pet animal who is being abused or neglected by its owner, call the police or the Humane Society and report what you know. Your complaint can be made anonymously, and your intervention may save the animal from a cruel and untimely death.

~ A properly managed zoo protects endangered species, like bald eagles, from becoming extinct, and at the same time helps people better understand and appreciate animals. Spend an afternoon at the nearest zoo and learn more about what you can do to help our animal friends.

~ Teach children to treat animals with respect, kindness and compassion. Studies have proven that many adult serial killers started their deadly careers as children, when they tortured and killed defenseless animals. When a child learns to be kind to animals, he or she learns to have respect for all forms of life.

~ The fur trade is alive and well, though not as much as in the past. As the public has become more and more aware of the cruel truth behind the fur industry, fewer and fewer people have wanted to wear anything made from fur. Still, some people have not quite gotten the point. When you see fur used in fashions in catalogues and magazines, write to the designer, the publisher of the magazine, or the store advertised in the catalog and let them know how you feel about the use of fur.

~ Birds usually eat well during the warmer seasons, but in winter, especially when it snows, it's hard for the ones who don't migrate to find food. Set up a bird feeder in your yard and keep it full year-round.

~ Have some old bath towels or blankets that are starting to get a little ratty around the edges? Don't throw them away—take them to your local animal shelter. The shelters can use them to line cages or dry the animals after a bath.

~ Refuse to buy from manufacturers who test their products on animals. The National Anti-Vivisection Society has published a handy guide, *Personal Care For Those Who Care*, listing hundreds of companies who do and do not use animals in product testing. Support the companies who are cruelty-free, and let those who aren't know that you won't buy anything from them until they stop testing on animals.

~ Everyone struggles when a region is plagued by drought, but wild animals suffer most. If you live in an area populated by deer, raccoons, squirrels, and other wild creatures, remember them if a drought should occur. Keep a bird bath or watering trough (a large bucket or flower box will do) filled with water so they can stay hydrated. A salt lick also helps during those dry times.

Help Our Planet

~ Does your school or workplace recycle? They should—but if they don't, you can start your own recycling program. You'll need containers (large plastic bins or garbage cans are perfect) for the recyclable materials, and these should be clearly labeled and placed in a high-traffic area. When the containers are full, haul the contents away to your local recycling center.

~ Complete the effects of recycling by purchasing recycled materials whenever possible. Many everyday items, from pencils to toilet paper, are made with at least some percentage of recycled content, so compare labels and support earth-friendly companies and products.

~ Take a trash walk. Equip yourself with a large garbage bag and take a walk around your neighborhood, through a park or wooded area, or along a stream. Collect all the litter you find along the way and dispose of it properly.

~ Exercise the authority of a voting citizen. Keep tabs on local elected officials and their attitudes toward the environment. Cast your vote for people who are committed to preserving our natural resources.

~ Plant a tree. A large shade tree planted near your home can reduce the amount of energy you need to spend on cooling it during the summer and heating it during the winter. It also captures air pollutants and transforms them into life-giving oxygen.

~ Turn off lights and electric appliances when you aren't using them. Reducing your own electricity consumption eases the strain on power plants and helps reduce the amount of pollution they generate.

~ Adopt a vacant piece of property. Clear it of trash and weeds, then plant trees, flowers, or even a vegetable garden. Make sure you get permission from the property owners first!

~ Whenever possible, avoid foam packaging. It's non-biodegradable, so for centuries it will continue to occupy landfill space. If you get foam peanuts in a package, reuse them in a package you send to someone else. Buy eggs in cardboard cartons, and recycle those when the eggs are gone.

~ Don't toss used batteries into the garbage. As the batteries break down, they release harmful chemicals like mercury into the soil, poisoning our groundwater supplies. Instead, find a recycling center that will take your batteries, or invest in a set of rechargeable batteries that can be used over and over.

~ Recycle your shopping bags. Paper bags can be recycled to make other necessary paper products without harvesting more trees. Many supermarket chains take plastic bags and recycle them to reduce waste; show your support for plastic bag recycling by patronizing those stores. Both paper and plastic bags can be reused many times.

~ Make your toilet more earth-friendly by finding a plastic bottle that fits inside your toilet tank. Fill it with water and position it where it won't block the flushing mechanism. You can also purchase toilet dams which have the same effect; both of these are good ways to reduce the amount of water your toilet uses with each flush.

~ The next time your car is dirty, don't pull out the garden hose, which can waste hundreds of gallons of water. Use a bucket and sponge if you have to wash it yourself. An even better idea is to take the car to a drive-through car wash, where the water is recycled—and it's much faster for you, too!

~ Check the faucets in your home and see to it that they shut off properly. A dripping faucet loses several gallons of water every day, which can be an expensive proposition as well as a waste of a precious resource.

~ Composting is a great way to reduce waste, and it's a lot simpler than you might think. A compost pile will turn everything from potato peelings to egg shells to grass clippings into rich, vitamin-laden soil, perfect for gardens. You can find directions for building and maintaining a compost pile on the Internet or in gardening manuals.

Help Work Toward World Peace

~ Think about the victims of hate crimes. People have been killed for hundreds of years because they were the "wrong" color or practiced the "wrong" religion or something else was "wrong" with them. Humans will always be different; remember that instead of trying to rid ourselves of our differences, we should learn to accept and appreciate them. How boring it would be if we were all the same!

~ Refrain from telling jokes based on ethnicity, religion, sexual preference, or skin color. Let others know that you don't want to hear such jokes told in your presence. Demeaning other people is never funny.

~ Make "Speak no evil" your personal motto. Get in the habit of *not* saying unkind things to or about others. Remember that you can't build yourself up by tearing someone else down.

~ Read books about a religion other than the one you practice. Attend services with a friend of a different faith, and invite them to attend one with you. Learning about someone else's belief system can help you better understand their point of view.

~ Learn a new language. Improving communication helps to foster international understanding and peace, and it can be a lot of fun too. This includes sign language!

~ Teach your children and other young people that *all* human beings deserve to be treated with respect, decency, and compassion. Attitudes learned in childhood can stay with a person for life; help kids learn to have the right attitude.

~ If you spot hate-oriented graffiti scrawled on a public place in your town, don't just ignore it—that implies that you agree with the person who wrote it. Report it to the proper authorities, and volunteer to help cover it with fresh paint.

~ Although outlawed in many countries, slavery is still practiced in several regions around the world. Find out which countries still have an active slave labor force, and refuse to purchase any products manufactured in that country.

~ Is a hate group planning a rally in your community? Plan an alternative event for your neighbors to draw attention away from them. The best weapon with which to combat hatred is love.

~ Write to your favorite artists, writers, musicians, actors and comedians and urge them to join the group Artists Against Racism. Encourage these celebrities to lend their famous names to the cause of peace and tolerance.

~ An organization called World Peace Day has a global celebration of peace every year on June 21st. If you live near a group that's planning to participate on the next Peace Day, get involved—it's a great way to meet people who share the goal of a more peaceful world. If there's no local celebration planned, consider spearheading one!

Some More Creative Ways to Help

~ The next time you have a party, picnic, or other get-together, sneak a bit of the spirit of giving into the festivities. Ask each of your guests to bring a nonperishable food item to donate to the local soup kitchen, or an article of gently used clothing to give to a homeless shelter.

~ Super-charge your birthday and holiday shopping list. Find out which charities your friends and family members would like to support, and make a donation on their behalf. Many charities will gladly send the gift recipient a card or letter explaining what will be done with the money that was given in his/her name. If you don't feel comfortable giving this kind of present, consider requesting that others do it for you on your birthday.

~ Have you been called on to plan a birthday party, bridal shower, or special anniversary bash for someone who would rather give than receive? Give them the best of both worlds by arranging a party at which the guests do something charitable. You can help build a new animal shelter, spend an afternoon cleaning up a stream, or host a Red Cross Bloodmobile. Figure out what kind of charity your guest of honor would most like to help, and take it from there.

~ If you've got your own site on the World Wide Web, you have a very handy tool for advocating change. Write about the issues and causes that interest you most. Provide links to other sites about those issues—Chapter Three will present many suggestions for this. Someone visiting your site may become inspired to get involved.

Chapter Three—Desktop Activism

There's never been anything quite like the Internet. It has thousands of places you can go in cyberspace to meet new friends, learn new things, or just be entertained.

What's great about this is that the Internet also provides the platform for a new kind of volunteering, which I like to call desktop activism. Without even leaving your home, you and that computer of yours can make valuable contributions to making our world a better place. There are hundreds of sites on the World Wide Web where you can add your name to a petition, donate to various charities, or simply educate yourself about a problem.

In the last chapter I suggested that, if you have your own site, you can use it to promote the causes you support by providing links to other sites with information. If you don't have your own site but would like one, you can probably set up one for yourself through your Internet provider. You can also get free, advertising-supported pages from several different sites; direct your browser to your preferred search engine and type in "free homepages" to find a provider.

I've taken the liberty of looking up several sites you might like to investigate as you roam the web. Each of these sites is overflowing with information about its specified subjects. Some have links to relevant online petitions;

some will allow you to join their mailing list, to receive "action alerts" in your e-mail—they'll send you a notice every time their site has something new you can do to help their cause.

To help humanity and work for a peaceful world

~ The Anti-Defamation League has formed a program, "Close the Book on Hate," which fights against hatred and intolerance, and at the same time promotes reading and literacy as weapons in that fight.
http://www.adl.org

~ Equality Now works for the safety, health, freedom and equality of women around the world.
http://www.equalitynow.org

~ The Fellowship of Reconciliation has been striving for peace and nonviolence since 1954.
http://www.forusa.org

~ iAbolish, the website of the American Anti-Slavery Society, provides information and ways that you can help stop slavery.
http://www.iabolish.com

~ SAFE (Stop Abuse For Everyone) has many suggestions on how anyone can help end the horrors of domestic violence.
http://www.safe4all.org

~ Save the World looks to improve the world by increasing volunteerism for many different causes.
http://www.speedweb2000.com/savetheworld

~ The Southern Poverty Law Center owns and operates two of the best sites for information about tolerance.
HateWatch—http://www.hatewatch.com
Tolerance.org—http://www.tolerance.org

~ The United States Freedom Corps provides a host of volunteer opportunities around the globe and in your own backyard.
http://www.freedomcorps.gov

~ The White Ribbon Campaign is being waged by men to end male violence against women.
http://www.whiteribbon.ca

Health-related links

If you have an interest in helping those whose lives have been affected by a specific physical or mental condition, or if you would like to learn more about a particular condition, you might want to examine some of the following sites:

AIDS/HIV—http://www.aids.org
Alcohol, drug, and other addictions—
http://www.spiritofrecovery.com
Alzheimer's disease—http://www.alzforum.org
Birth defects—http://www.modimes.org
Blindness—http://www.iefusa.org
Cancer (all forms)—http://www.cancer.org
Cystic Fibrosis—http://www.CysticFibrosis.com
Deafness—http://www.nad.org
Endometriosis—http://www.EndometriosisAssn.org

Fibromyalgia—http://www.fmnetnews.com
Heart diseases—http://www.heartpoint.com
Multiple Sclerosis—http://www.msworld.org
Muscular Dystrophy—
    http://www.muscular-dystrophy.org
Organ donation—http://www.transweb.org
Parkinson's disease—http://www.pdf.org
Suicide prevention—http://www.yellowribbon.org

If the condition which interests you doesn't appear on the list, try one of these health directories:
    WebMD Health—http://my.webmd.com
    Healthfinder—http://www.healthfinder.gov
    You can also check the Health section at Yahoo!—
        http://www.yahoo.com

Helping animals and the planet

~ In the spirit of their founder, the National Audubon Society seeks to preserve our natural heritage.
http://www.audubon.org

~ Care2 is a huge organization working largely for the environment, but also for other causes as well.
http://www.care2.com

~ The Defenders of Wildlife want to save the endangered species of the world.
http://www.defenders.org

~ The Doris Day Animal Foundation wants to create a more compassionate relationship between people and animals.
http://www.ddaf.org

~ Forests.org, Inc. is looking to bring an end to deforestation and protect our old-growth forests.
http://forests.org

~ Oceans At Risk (also called Oceana) works to protect the world's oceans and marine life.
http://www.oceansatrisk.com

~ The Wilderness Society wants to preserve the last "great places" in America.
http://www.wilderness.org

~ The World Wildlife Foundation has a program, the Panda Passport, that lets you take all kinds of actions. You can send letters to government officials and colorful e-cards to your friends.
http://passport.panda.org

There is another kind of site on the web that will let you help the causes you support, and it's incredibly easy. These sites and programs have made a special arrangement with advertisers and other sponsors. Every time a visitor clicks on a designated graphic on the website, the sponsors make a monetary donation to the charity in question. Add them to your personal bookmarks, and try to visit whenever you log onto the Internet; the cost to *you* is nothing but a few seconds of your time.

To help other people

Donate a minute of free hospital care to a child.
http://www.giveaminute.org

Raise money for various cancer charities.
http://www.cancercharities.com

Help raise money for breast cancer treatment and prevention.
http://www.thebreastcancersite.com
http://breastcancer.care2.com

Help flood disaster victims.
http://www.causeaneffect.org

Raise money to help clear landmines.
http://www.clearlandmines.com

Support humanitarian volunteer work.
http://www.thehumanitariansite.org

Help Brazilian families reach economic stability, so their children can go to school instead of work.
http://www.clickfome.com.br/english/index.html

Provide medical treatment and preventive care to underprivileged children.
http://www.thechildhealthsite.com

Provide food for starving people.
http://www.againsthunger.org
http://www.hungrychildren.com

http://www.stopthehunger.com/hunger
http://www.thehungersite.com

To help animals and the environment

Protect over 150 square feet of land from deforestation.
http://www.ecologyfund.com

Help reduce global warming.
http://www.environmentsite.com

Donate money to the Clean Air Conservancy.
http://www.iwantcleanair.com

Plant a tree in the Brazilian rain forest. (Note: this site is entirely in Spanish)
http://www.tree4life.com

Help an abandoned or abused animal.
http://www.theanimalrescuesite.com

Preserve rain forest land.
http://www.therainforestsite.com

Visit all of Care2's ongoing "races" for the planet:
To protect the big cats—http://bigcats.care2.com
To protect giant pandas—http://panda.care2.com
To protect the rain forest—http://rainforest.care2.com
To protect the oceans—http://oceans.care2.com

The following sites allow you to choose from multiple causes to support. If you have the time, you can browse and make a donation to all the causes listed.

Free Donation—http://www.freedonation.com
We Did—http://www.wedid.net
Charity Click—http://www.electract-bardon.co.uk
Click and Save—http://clickandsave.8k.com
Digital Charity—http://www.digitalcharity.com

You may decide to add some real-world volunteering to your desktop activism, if you haven't already. There are some great sites on the web that can help you find ways to get involved in your own community:

Volunteer Match—http://www.volunteermatch.com
One World—http://www.oneworld.net
Idealist—http://www.idealist.org
Helping—http://www.helping.org
Mentoring—http://www.mentoring.org
SERVEnet—http://www.servenet.org

Chapter Four—Be a Great Volunteer

You're just about ready to roll here. You've decided what kind of volunteering you want to do, you've brainstormed ideas, you've turned to the Internet for information and advice. Before you get started with your project, however, I've thought of some things that we should discuss first. This chapter is mostly full of common sense stuff, but it never hurts to have these things repeated.

You may have noticed that during the Workbook section, I used the word *comfortable* a lot. Some people would argue with me that volunteering isn't supposed to be comfortable, but let's be honest. If you were faced with the prospect of doing something really unpleasant, and you knew you didn't have to do it, do you think you still would? A lot of people wouldn't. That's why it's so important to tailor your volunteering experience to your own talents, abilities, beliefs, and interests. If you believe in a cause and enjoy what you're doing, you're going to want to keep doing it.

There are lots of different reasons for getting involved with public service. Some do it because it looks good on a resume or college application; some groups, like the National Honor Society in many high schools, require that their members perform a certain number of hours of volunteer work. Some believe very strongly in the mission statement of the organization with which they're working. Some just really like the good feeling that comes from helping others. Whatever your reasons for doing it, the fact remains that you are making a commitment. You are dedicating your time and energy to a cause which is important to you. Even though you aren't being paid for your volunteer work, you should treat this commitment with the same responsibility and devotion that you would a paying job. If you get sick or an emergency comes up, show your team members or the organization for whom you're volunteering the same courtesy you'd be required to show your boss. Get any necessary telephone numbers ahead of time, and if you can't show up when you've said you will, call and explain.

Remember—especially when doing solo projects—to get any permission you'll need to go ahead with your plans. If you're going to be on private property, speak to the owner first. Even if you're doing your volunteering on public grounds or your own property, it's never a bad idea to talk to the local police or a member of your town council about what you'll be doing; you might find out, for instance, that you need a permit. Most importantly, if anyone working on the project is underage, make sure you have permission from parents or guardians before you even get started.

Be prepared for the project. Some volunteering, such as with hospital candy striper programs, requires a uniform. If you're working with an organization, find out in advance how you should dress. Learn the correct phrases to use if you should have to answer the phone or greet office visitors. If you think it will help, take notes; keep a small notebook and pen in your pocket for handy referrals.

When working on an outdoor project, like participating in a beach cleanup or building low-income housing, you'll have a completely different dress code than your office counterpart. Old jeans, t-shirts and sweats are best. You should also wear work gloves, to protect your hands from blisters as well as from things like poison ivy. A baseball cap is a good idea; the brim will shade your face from the sun, and if your hair is long, you can tie it back through the cap. Bring sunscreen with you, and reapply it often to prevent sunburn. Water is essential—you'll be working up a sweat out there, so keep your water bottle close at hand.

If you're coordinating a volunteer project with your friends, and not operating through an established association, you'll need to take care of the details that an organization might otherwise handle. Talk to each of your friends and find out if there's anything you need to know; make sure they all understand what's involved in your project. If anyone has special considerations—for instance, they're on prescription medication or use an asthma inhaler—make sure they bring or do whatever is necessary. As project coordinator, you should pack and bring along a small first aid kit for the team. Include things like adhesive bandages, aspirin, disinfectant, calamine lotion, sunscreen, and change for the pay phone. There's never a charge for dialing 9-1-1 in an emergency, but include the change in case someone needs to call home, or else have someone bring along a cell phone. Arrange for the group to take breaks frequently enough to suit everyone, and make sure they all get plenty of water. Don't forget to congratulate everyone at the end for a job well done!

Your volunteer project may bring you into contact with the media. If you're the one planning the project, you might want to get in touch with your local newspapers, radio stations, and television networks to advertise what you're doing and why; the media coverage can generate public interest in your cause. Be prepared ahead of time for questions they may ask, and have an idea of the answers you'll give. If you're with an organization, they usually have a designated spokesperson whose job is to deal with reporters, so find out who this is and refer any media questions to him or her.

Finally, remember to have *fun* with your volunteer work. That's not a license to goof off—always keep in mind that what you're doing is very important. The cause you're supporting is bound to be serious, and deserving of your maturity and responsibility. But that doesn't mean you can't enjoy yourself. Perhaps you can play music while you work, or arrange a weekend ball game for the people working with you. Ask your friends and family members to come and volunteer with you, and reach out to new friends in your public service field. When you're "off duty" with a project, invite your team members to get something to eat and get to know each other better. You can create for each other a much-needed network of support; and when you work with friends, the work becomes much more enjoyable. Never forget the importance of what you're doing...but never forget that it's important to enjoy life too.

Chapter Five—Contact Information

Here are mailing addresses, telephone numbers, and website addresses for many different organizations who can help you with your volunteering. All of the groups who were mentioned in the ideas section are listed here, along with several others, in alphabetical order. Except where indicated, all the organizations on this list are located in the United States.

I sincerely regret that I had to limit myself in the number of organizations I put into this book, as there are so many more who deserve inclusion. I tried to cover as many different kinds of causes as I could. If you can't find what you need in this chapter, or if you want to go in search of more, try your phone book for resources in your area. You can also check your local newspaper, especially the Sunday edition; many papers carry information about volunteer programs.

AIDS Action
1906 Sunderland Place NW
Washington, DC 20036
http://www.aidsaction.org
This is a network of over 3,000 national organizations committed to the fight against AIDS. They're a great source

of information on how you can help those who have been infected with the HIV virus.

Alliance for Families and Children
11700 West Lake Park Drive
Milwaukee, WI 53224
1-800-221-3726
http://www.alliance1.org
    The AFC helps needy families in more than 2,000 communities, and can direct you to volunteer programs in your own area.

The American Anti-Slavery Society
198 Tremont Street, #421
Boston, MA 02116
1-800-884-0719
http://www.iabolish.org
    Partly because of their efforts, more than 45,000 slaves around the world have been freed since 1993.

American Cancer Society
1599 Clifton Road NE
Atlanta, GA 30329
1-800-ACS-2345
http://www.cancer.org
    The ACS is the United States' foremost organization for battling cancer through education and action.

American Council of the Blind
1155 Fifteenth Street NW, Suite 1004
Washington, DC 20005
1-800-424-8666
http://www.acb.org

This organization can help you if you're interested in working to help the blind and visually impaired.

American Heart Association
7272 Greenville Avenue
Dallas, TX 75231
(214) 373-6300
http://www.americanheart.org
The American Heart Association can provide you with plenty of information on how you can help prevent all kinds of heart disease.

The American Red Cross
431 18th Street NW
Washington, DC 20006
(202) 639-3520
http://www.redcross.org
Contact them for information on giving blood, making donations, and volunteer opportunities around the world.

American Society for the Prevention of Cruelty to Animals (ASPCA)
424 East 92nd Street
New York, NY 10128
(212) 876-7700
http://www.aspca.org
Although the only volunteer opportunities within the ASPCA itself are at the headquarters in New York, they can help you find animal shelters in your area where your services will be welcome.

AmeriCares
161 Cherry Street
New Canaan, CT 06840
1-800-486-4357
http://www.americares.org
AmeriCares reaches out around the world in a variety of programs, offering emergency disaster relief and humanitarian aid.

Artists Against Racism (AAR International)
Box 54511
Toronto, Ontario, Canada M5M 4N5
http://www.artistsagainstracism.org
Learn which celebrities are involved in this campaign to promote tolerance and end racial discord, and how you can help them.

The Box Project, Inc.
P.O. Box 435
87 East Street
Plainville, CT 06062
1-800-268-9928
http://www.boxproject.org
The Box Project matches needy families with sponsor families who provide monthly gifts of material goods, as well as friendship and encouragement.

Campaign for Tobacco-Free Kids
1707 L Street NW, Suite 800
Washington, DC 20036
(202) 296-5469
http://www.tobaccofreekids.org

This group wants to bring a complete halt to the purchase and use of tobacco products by children and teenagers.

Covenant House
460 West 41st Street
New York, NY 10036
(212) 613-0300
http://www.covenanthouse.org
This international organization provides shelter and a future for homeless youth.

Fellowship of Reconciliation
521 N. Broadway
Nyack, NY 10960
(845) 358-4601
http://www.forusa.org
The oldest and largest interfaith peace group in the United States, FOR is working to end violence, intolerance, and war.

Food For All
3246 Prospect Street NW
Washington, DC 20007
1-800-896-5101
http://www.foodforall.org
Find out which supermarket chains will let you help this organization in its fight to end world hunger.

Habitat For Humanity International
121 Habitat Street
Americus, GA 31709
http://www.habitat.org
Help construct sturdy, affordable housing for impoverished

people around the world.

The Humane Society of the United States
2100 L Street NW
Washington DC 20037
(202) 452-1100
http://www.hsus.org
The Humane Society is a multinational task force of people committed to a truly compassionate world, where animals and people live in harmony.

Keep America Beautiful
1010 Washington Boulevard
Stamford, CT 06901
(203) 323-8987
http://www.kab.org

This group focuses its energies on stamping out pollution, and encourages recycling in communities.

Landmark Volunteers
P.O. Box 455
Sheffield, MA 01257
(413) 229-0255
http://www.volunteers.com
This organization places high school students in summer volunteer programs with different institutions across the country.

Lions Clubs International Headquarters
300 West 22nd Street
Oak Brook, IL 60523-8842
http://www.lionsclubs.org

The Lions have local chapters around the world who work to help disaster victims, assist the blind and elderly, and improve communities through leadership.

Literacy Volunteers of America
635 James Street
Syracuse, NY 13203
(315) 472-0001
http://www.literacyvolunteers.org
This organization can help you find a local program if you want to teach others how to read.

Locks of Love
2925 10th Avenue North, Suite 102
Lake Worth, FL 33461
1-888-896-1588
http://www.locksoflove.org
This nonprofit group takes donations of cut-off hair and turns them into wigs and hairpieces for children whose own hair has fallen out due to medical problems.

March of Dimes
1275 Mamaroneck Avenue
White Plains, NY 10605
1-888-663-4637
http://www.modimes.org
The MoD fights to prevent birth defects and bring healthy babies into the world. Find out how you can participate in their annual walk-a-thon fundraiser.

Meals on Wheels Association of America
1-800-677-1116
http://www.projectmeal.org
Meals on Wheels provides hot, nutritious meals to senior citizens and shut-ins all over America. Call their information line to find your local chapter.

The National Anti-Vivisection Society
53 West Jackson Boulevard, Suite 1552
Chicago, IL 60604
1-800-888-NAVS
http://www.navs.org
Ask for a copy of their book, *Personal Care for Those Who Care*, and learn more about product testing on animals.

The National Center for Missing and Exploited Children
Charles B. Wang International Children's Building
699 Prince Street
Alexandria, VA 22314
(703) 274-3900
http://www.missingkids.com
The Center seeks to reunite kidnap victims and runaways with their families. They have many different, easy programs with which you can become involved.

National Coalition Against Domestic Violence
P.O. Box 18749
Denver, CO 80218
(303) 839-1852
http://www.ncadv.org
The Coalition is working to fulfill their motto: "Every home a safe home." They can help you if you'd like to assist victims of

domestic violence.

National Coalition for the Homeless
1012 14th Street NW, Suite 600
Washington, DC 20005
(202) 737-6444
http://nch.ari.net
This organization offers many different ways in which you can help the homeless.

National Council on the Aging
409 Third Street SW
Washington, DC 20024
(202) 479-1200
http://www.ncoa.org
If you're interested in volunteering with senior citizens, this organization can give you lots of ideas.

National Crime Prevention Council
1000 Connecticut Avenue NW, 13th Floor
Washington, DC 20036
(202) 466-6272
http://www.ncpc.org
If you'd like to start a neighborhood watch, or find other ways to prevent crime in your local area, McGruff the crime dog and his human partners would be glad to help.

Oxfam America
26 West Street
Boston, MA 02111
1-800-77OXFAM
http://www.oxfamamerica.org

Oxfam is a very active group committed to fighting poverty, hunger, and social injustice all over the world.

RAINN (Rape, Abuse, and Incest National Network)
635-B Pennsylvania Avenue SE
Washington, DC 20003
1-800-656-4673, extension 3
http://www.rainn.org
The largest organization of its kind in the United States, they can help you find information if you're interested in helping the victims of sexual abuse or assault.

Rebuilding Together
1536 16th Street NW
Washington, DC 20036-1042
1-800-4-REHAB-9
http://www.rebuildingtogether.org
The Home Depot has teamed up with Christmas in April to repair and rebuild low-income housing and neighborhoods.

St. Jude's Ranch for Children
100 St. Jude's Street
Boulder City, NV 89005-1618
1-800-492-3562
http://www.stjudesranch.org
Send your used greeting cards to the abused children at St. Jude's Ranch, and they can earn college money by turning them into new cards to sell.

The Salvation Army
1025 F Street NE
Washington, DC 20002

(202) 783-0233

http://www.salvationarmy.org

From its beginnings, the Salvation Army has focused on helping the poor and homeless in any way they can.

Special Olympics

1325 G Street NW, Suite 500

Washington, DC 20005

(202) 628-3630

http://www.specialolympics.org

This organization helps people with mental and physical limitations participate in sports and athletic competitions.

United Way of America

701 North Fairfax Street

Alexandria, VA 22314

(703) 836-7112

http://www.unitedway.org

This national organization has many local chapters across the country, working to help disadvantaged people in a variety of ways.

Volunteers of America

1660 Duke Street

Alexandria, VA 22314

(703) 341-5000

http://www.voa.org

This group has many service programs across the country with which you can become involved, and also offers suggestions for solo volunteering projects.

The Wilderness Society
1615 M Street NW
Washington, DC 20036
1-800-843-9453
http://www.wilderness.org
This organization of committed environmentalists seeks to preserve America's last wild lands, as well as find alternative solutions to the problems threatening those lands.

The Wireless Foundation—Call to Protect
c/o Motorola
1580 East Ellsworth Road
Ann Arbor, MI 48108
http://www.wirelessfoundation.org/12give/index2.cfm
Donate used cellular phones to victims of domestic violence.

World Peace and Prayer Day
P.O. Box 952
Hill City, SD 57745
http://www.worldpeaceday.com
Get involved with this group's annual celebration of peace and nonviolence.

World Wildlife Fund
1250 24th Street NE
Washington, DC 20037
(202) 293-4800
http://www.worldwildlife.org
Find out how you can help save endangered animals and wild lands all around the world.

Yellow Ribbon Suicide Prevention Program
P.O. Box 644
Westminster, CO 80036-0644
(303) 429-3530
http://www.yellowribbon.org

The Yellow Ribbon program, organized by the family and friends of a young man who committed suicide, is reaching out to save others from ending their own lives.

Chapter Six—More Material

I hope that this book has provided you with a lot of the information you were seeking. If you'd like to read other books that can give you some great ideas about volunteer projects, I suggest any of the following:

Berry, R. J., editor. *The Care of Creation.*

Coplin, William D., PhD. *How You Can Help: An Easy Guide to Doing Good Deeds in Your Everyday Life.*

The EarthWorks Group. *50 Simple Things You Can Do to Save the Earth; The Next Step: 50 More Things You Can Do to Save the Earth;* and *50 Simple Things Kids Can Do to Save the Earth.*

Galla, Preston. *The Complete Idiot's Guide to Volunteering for Teens.*

Gould, Meredith. *Deliberate Acts of Kindness: Service as a Spiritual Practice.*

Kasich, John. *Courage is Contagious: Ordinary People Doing Extraordinary Things to Change the Face of America.*

Raynolds, John, with Gene Stone. *The Halo Effect: How Volunteering Can Lead to a More Fulfilling Life and a Better Career.*

Stern-LaRosa, Caryl, and Ellen Bofheimer Bettman. *Hate Hurts*, published by the Anti-Defamation League.

Awards

Do you know someone who has gone above and beyond the call of duty with his or her volunteering? Of course, when someone sets out to be a volunteer, they don't really do it with the expectation of getting recognized for their efforts—but let's be honest, it's always nice! There are some national awards out there for volunteers who have really gone the distance for their chosen causes, so if you'd like to nominate someone for one of them, here's the contact information.

The Jefferson Award and the President's Student Service Award
    The American Institute for Public Service
    100 West 10th Street, Suite 215
    Wilmington, DE 19801
    (302) 622-9101
    http://www.aips.org

The Spirit of Hope Award and the Ron G. Bliss Award
    American Hope
    P.O. Box 53738
    Houston, TX 77052-3738
    (877) 879-9537
    http://www.americanhope.org

Words of Wisdom

There come days for me, and I don't doubt that you've had similar experiences, when I wonder if it's really worth it to keep doing what I do. Sometimes it can be very hard to be a volunteer. Other people seem like they don't care, or the tasks to be accomplished appear very daunting. On days like these, I pull out this list of quotations and remind myself that I really am doing something important, even if nobody gives me any credit for doing it. I'd like to share that list with you, for the days when you need some extra inspiration.

"We must use time wisely and forever realize that the time is always ripe to do right."—Nelson Mandela

"Never doubt that a small group of thoughtful, committed citizens can change the world. Indeed, it's the only thing that ever has."—Margaret Mead

"You must be the change you wish to see in the world."—Mahatma Gandhi

"It is not fair to ask of others what you are not willing to do yourself."—Eleanor Roosevelt

"Darkness cannot drive out darkness; only light can do that. Hate cannot drive out hate; only love can do that."—Martin Luther King, Jr.

"There is always something to do. There are hungry people to feed, naked people to clothe, sick people to comfort and make

well. And while I don't expect you to save the world, I do think it's not asking too much to love those with whom you sleep, share the happiness of those whom you call friend, engage those among you who are visionary and remove from your life those who offer you depression, despair and disrespect."—Nikki Giovanni

"It's kind of fun to do the impossible."—Walt Disney

Tell me your story!

I'd love to hear all about your volunteer experience. Whether you serve regularly with a national organization or you jumped in on a grassroots project, I'd be delighted to know how volunteering has affected your life. Have you succeeded in your goals? Did you ultimately make a difference?

I most especially would be interested to hear about projects that got their start from ideas you dreamed up while reading my book. But even if you started your volunteering before I ever began writing this, I'd like to know your story. If I get enough good, inspiring true stories of the volunteer spirit, I might just have to write another book and share them with the world!

Feel free to contact me via e-mail at volunteerspirit@juno.com, or by dropping a letter in the mail and sending it to:

Laura Klotz
P.O. Box 124
Catasauqua, PA 18032

I look forward to hearing from you! My best wishes to you with your volunteer projects, now and in the future.

* * * * *

About the author

Laura Klotz has been writing since she was nine years old, when her first story was "published" via her grandparents' carbon copy machine. She has been volunteering in one capacity or another since high school, when she worked as a hospital candy striper; more than ten years of public service experience led her to write Saving the World in Your Spare Time. *When not actively pursuing a volunteer project, she works for the federal government as a data processor and "Director of Office Morale." She shares a small house in Pennsylvania's beautiful Lehigh Valley with her husband, Kevin, and two very spoiled cats. This is her first book.*

Printed in the United States
1515100001B/19